Scriptural Rosary

*A Modern Version of the Way
the Rosary was Once Prayed
Throughout Western Europe
in the Late Middle Ages*

Illustrated by Virginia Broderick

Christianica (America)
1807 Prairie Street
P.O. Box 685
Glenview, IL 60025

Christianica (Europa)
8, rue de Kahler
L-8378 Kleinbettingen
Luxembourg

Nihil Obstat:
Rt. Rev. Msgr. John A. McMahon
Censor Librorum

Imprimatur:
✠ Albert Cardinal Meyer
Archbishop of Chicago

L. C. Catalog Card Number: 64-66463
ISBN: 0-911346-01-5

Excerpts from The Jerusalem Bible
copyright © 1966 by Darton, Longman &
Todd, Ltd. and Doubleday and Company, Inc.
Used by permission of the publisher

37 38 39 40 41 42 43 98 97 96 95 94 93 92

What the Scriptural Rosary Is

The *Scriptural Rosary* is a modern version of the way the Rosary was once prayed throughout Western Christendom in the late Middle Ages.

In those times—about 1425 to 1525 A.D. —people recited a different little thought, or meditation, as they prayed each Hail Mary of the Rosary. These thoughts for each Hail Mary bead described some event or incident in the lives of Jesus and Mary.

The new *Scriptural Rosary* presented here follows this old medieval custom of assigning a different little thought to each Hail Mary bead. The thoughts have been arranged so that the story of each Mystery unfolds, bead-by-bead, in ten consecutive steps. Most importantly, the *Scriptural Rosary* draws its Hail Mary thoughts directly from the inspired writings of the New and Old Testaments. This was not done in the Middle Ages. It is for this reason that this new version of the medieval way of praying the

Rosary is called the *'Scriptural' Rosary:* because 147 of the 150 little Hail Mary thoughts are direct quotations from the scriptures.

Why the Scriptural Rosary Is Important

If you have sometimes found it difficult to keep thinking about the Mysteries as you pray each decade of the Rosary, then the *Scriptural Rosary* may be very helpful.

Since the *Scriptural Rosary* distributes the story of each Mystery, bead-by-bead, over the entire decade, you will find that you are never more than one Hail Mary away from a vivid, thought-provoking reference to one of the Mystery stories.

You are likely to discover, as did the people of the Middle Ages, that the bead-by-bead method of meditation can help to increase the devotional impact of the Rosaries you pray. For as our mind becomes more attentive to the profound messages of the Mysteries, we are more likely to appreciate what they contain, follow what they advise, and obtain what they promise.

How to Pray
the Scriptural Rosary

For an Individual

Let us say that you are about to pray the Fourth Joyful Mystery, The Presentation. You should first pray the Our Father while thinking about the general significance of The Presentation.

Then, before praying the first Hail Mary, read the scriptural quotation which applies to the first Hail Mary bead:

Observing the Law of Moses, they took
Jesus up to Jerusalem/
to present him to the Lord.

Luke 2:22

Hail ✡ Mary

Picture this scene in your mind and think about its meaning and significance while you pray the first Hail Mary.

Then read the scriptural quotation for the second Hail Mary bead, which says:

Now in Jerusalem there was a man named Simeon./

He was an upright and devout man.

Luke 2:25

Hail ✡ Mary

Think of this second scene in the story of The Presentation while you pray the second Hail Mary.

Continue in this way for each of the remaining beads of the decade.

For Two People or a Group

The *Scriptural Rosary* has also been arranged as a balanced, alternating prayer. Each scriptural quotation is divided into two distinct parts: a beginning part for the first person or leader to recite, and a response for the second person, or the rest of the group. The division between the two parts is shown by a slash mark (/).

This format enables two people, or a group of people, to pray the *Scriptural Rosary* in the same familiar form that is used to recite the Angelus: (The angel of the Lord declared unto Mary./ And she conceived of the Holy Spirit. Hail Mary . . .)

8

Historic Background
of the
Scriptural Rosary

The story of how the Rosary of the Blessed Virgin Mary originated, and how it has developed and changed over the centuries, is one of the most interesting but little known chapters of the history of our Faith. A brief look at this curious story will show that the *Scriptural Rosary* presented here is actually very similar to the form of Rosary that was once in universal use during the late Middle Ages.

An Outgrowth of the
150 Psalms of David

Most historians trace the origin of the Rosary as we know it today back to the so-called Dark Ages of ninth century Ireland. In those days, as is still true today, the 150 Psalms of David were one of the most important forms of monastic prayer. Monks recited or chanted the Psalms day-after-day as a major source of inspiration.

The lay people who lived near the monasteries could see the beauty of this devotion, but because very few people outside the monasteries knew how to read in those days, and because the 150 Psalms are too long to memorize, the lay people were unable to adapt this prayer form for their own use.

So one day in about the year 800 A.D., one of the Irish monks suggested to the neighboring lay people that they might like to pray a series of 150 Our Fathers in place of the 150 Psalms. Little did he know that his simple suggestion was the first step in the development of what would one day become the most popular non-liturgical prayer form of Christianity.

At first, in order to count their 150 Our Fathers, people carried around leather pouches which held 150 pebbles. Soon they advanced to ropes with 150 or 50 knots; and eventually they began to use strings with 50 pieces of wood.

Shortly afterwards the clergy and lay people in other parts of Europe began to recite, as a repetitive prayer, the Angelic Salutation, which makes up most of the first part of our Hail Mary. St. Peter Damian, who died in 1072, was the first to mention this prayer form. Soon many people were praying the fifty Angelic Salutations while others favored the fifty Our Fathers.

Origin of the Mysteries

Then during the thirteenth century another prayer form, which would soon give the Rosary its Mysteries, began to develop. Many medieval theologians had long considered the 150 Psalms to be veiled prophecies about the life, death, and resurrection of Jesus. By deep meditation and skillful interpretation of the Psalms certain of these men began to compose 'Psalters of Our Lord and Savior Jesus Christ.' These were series of 150 praises in honor of Jesus, based upon interpretations of the 150 Psalms.

Soon 'psalters' devoted to 150 praises of Mary were also composed. When a psalter of Marian praises numbered 50 instead of 150 it was commonly called a 'rosarium,' or bouquet.

Thus, during the thirteenth century there were four distinct 'psalters' in use at the same time: the 150 Our Fathers, the 150 Angelic Salutations, the 150 praises of Jesus, and the 150 praises of Mary. In an age when unity

11

was held in such high regard, perhaps it was inevitable that these four prayer forms should eventually be combined.

The Carthusians Combine Prayers and Mysteries

The first step toward the combination of these four kinds of psalters came in about 1365 A.D. when Henry of Kalkar, the Visitator of the Carthusian Order, grouped the 150 Angelic Salutations into decades and put an Our Father before each decade. This combined the Our Father and the Hail Mary for the first time.

Next, in about 1409, another Carthusian, Dominic the Prussian, wrote a book which attached a psalter of fifty thoughts about the lives of Jesus and Mary to a Rosary of 50 Hail Marys. This was the first time that a special thought was ever provided for each Hail Mary bead. Eventually the 50 Hail Mary thoughts of Dominic the Prussian were divided, as Henry of Kalkar had done, into groups of ten with an Our Father in between. Many variations of this form were composed between about 1425 and 1470, but the changes were gradual, not sudden.

12

The Dominicans Popularize the Special Hail Mary Thoughts

By 1470, when the Dominican Alan of Rupe founded the first Rosary Confraternity, and thereby launched the Dominican Order as the foremost missionaries of the Rosary, he could refer to the Rosary with a special thought for each Hail Mary bead (which was the form he favored) as the 'new' Rosary, while he referred to the form with the Hail Marys and no accompanying statements as the 'old' Rosary.

Through the efforts of Alan of Rupe and the early Dominicans this prayer form—150 Hail Marys with a special thought for each bead—spread rapidly throughout Western Christendom.

It is important to note that this form of Rosary—the form which Alan of Rupe promoted so successfully as the Rosary of St. Dominic—is the model upon which the new *Scriptural Rosary* is based, that is, a Rosary with a special thought for each of the 150 Hail Mary beads.

But the fifteenth century was a time of change and this successful medieval Rosary

13

form was gradually abandoned as the Christian world moved out of the Middle Ages and into the Renaissance.

Picture Rosaries Introduce the Short Rosary We Use Today

The abandonment of the medieval Rosary form, the form which provided a special thought for each Hail Mary bead, came about in this manner: In about 1500 it became possible to reproduce woodcut picture prints inexpensively for the first time. Since the vast majority of people still could not read, these picture Rosaries became immediately popular. But since it was difficult and expensive to draw and print 150 different pictures, one for each Hail Mary thought in the medieval Rosary, the new picture Rosaries usually showed only fifteen pictures—one for each Our Father bead. At first the ten Hail Mary thoughts were printed around each Our Father picture. Perhaps the most beautiful picture Rosary of this sort was the one first published in Venice by Alberto da Castello, O.P., in 1521. But during the 16th and 17th centuries the use of the special Hail Mary thoughts gradually died out, and there

14

remained only the fifteen brief Our Father thoughts which have survived as the fifteen Mysteries we know today.

(As an interesting historical footnote, the only place in the world where the old medieval Rosary with 150 Hail Mary thoughts is known to survive today is in the isolated little mountain village of Schröcken, high in the Vorarlberg Alps of Austria. Here the

villagers still come together as they have since the Middle Ages to pray the Rosary the way it was once prayed throughout the Christian world.)

As soon as the short Rosary of fifteen Mysteries and no Hail Mary thoughts had re-

15

placed the medieval form, people recognized the need to augment the fifteen brief Mystery statements. Supplementary prayers usually took the form of narratives or meditations to be read before praying each decade. One of the most popular of these sets of fifteen meditations was written by St. Louis de Montfort in about 1700. Most of the currently popular novena meditations follow this format, that is, an introductory paragraph of devotional thoughts to be read before praying each decade.

First Stirrings of a Return to the Medieval Rosary Form

Then beginning in the early 20th century, there appeared the first signs of a return to the medieval method. Provost Walter of Innichen published a series of thoughts for each Hail Mary in German. In 1920 Father Kilian Baumer composed another series of Hail Mary meditations which were published in Fribourg, Switzerland. The most recent printed work with special thoughts for each Hail Mary is that of Dr. Magnus Seng, a Canadian surgeon, published in 1946.

Each of these recent writers composed pertinent statements, or thoughts, to be read before or after praying each Hail Mary of the Rosary.

The *Scriptural Rosary* presented here differs from these recent compositions, as it differs from the medieval version, in that it is composed almost entirely of direct quotations from the scriptures. These quotations are blended to tell the story of each Mystery in ten consecutive thoughts.

This brief review of the historical development of the Rosary should serve to show that the *Scriptural Rosary* is actually nothing more than an application of the scriptures to the way the Rosary was once prayed throughout Western Christendom in the late Middle Ages.

If this modern version of the old 15th century Rosary serves to improve the quality of the meditations of a few hundred people in the 20th century, then this book will have fulfilled its objectives handsomely.

1960

The Scriptural Rosary

In the name of the Father, and of the Son, and of the Holy Spirit./   Amen.

I believe in God, the Father almighty, Creator of heaven and earth; and in Jesus Christ, his only Son, our Lord; who was conceived by the Holy Spirit, born of the Virgin Mary, suffered under Pontius Pilate, was crucified, died, and was buried. He descended into hell; the third day he rose again from the dead; he ascended into heaven, sits at the right hand of God, the Father almighty; from there he shall come to judge the living and the dead./

I believe in the Holy Spirit, the holy Catholic Church, the communion of saints, the forgiveness of sins, the resurrection of the body, and life everlasting. Amen.

Our Father who art in heaven, hallowed be thy name; thy kingdom come; thy will be done, on earth as it is in heaven./

Give us this day our daily bread; and forgive us our trespasses, as we forgive those who trespass against us; and lead us not into temptation, but deliver us from evil. Amen.

Hail, Mary, full of grace, the Lord is with you; blessed are you among women, and blessed is the fruit of your womb, Jesus./

Holy Mary, Mother of God, pray for us sinners, now and at the hour of our death. Amen. (Three times)

Glory be to the Father, and to the Son, and to the Holy Spirit./

As it was in the beginning, is now, and ever shall be, world without end. Amen.

First Joyful Mystery
THE ANNUNCIATION
Our 🌹 Father

The angel Gabriel was sent by God to a
    virgin;/
  and the virgin's name was Mary.

Luke 1:26, 27

Hail 🌹 Mary

'Rejoice, so highly favored!/
  The Lord is with you.'

Luke 1:28

Hail 🌹 Mary

She was deeply disturbed by these
    words/
  and asked herself what this greeting
  could mean.

Luke 1:29

Hail 🌹 Mary

But the angel said to her, 'Mary, do
not be afraid;/
you have won God's favor.'

Luke 1:30

Hail Mary

'Listen! You are to conceive and bear
a son,/
and you must name him Jesus.'

Luke 1:31

Hail Mary

'He will be great and will be called
Son of the Most High;/
and his reign will have no end.'

Luke 1:32, 33

Hail Mary

Mary said to the angel, 'But how can
this come about,/
since I am a virgin?'

Luke 1:34

Hail Mary

'The Holy Spirit will come upon you/
and the power of the Most High will
cover you with its shadow.'

Luke 1:35

Hail ❀ Mary

'And so the child will be holy/
and will be called Son of God.'

Luke 1:35

Hail ❀ Mary

'I am the handmaid of the Lord,' said
Mary/
'let what you have said be done to me.'

Luke 1:38

Hail ❀ Mary

Glory be to the Father, and to the Son,
and to the Holy Spirit./ As it was
in the beginning, is now,
and ever shall be,
world without
end. Amen.

Second Joyful Mystery
THE VISITATION
Our ✝ Father

Mary set out at that time and went to
the hill country./
And she went into Zechariah's house
and greeted Elizabeth.

Luke 1:39, 40

Hail ✝ Mary

Now as soon as Elizabeth heard Mary's
greeting, the child leaped in her
womb/
and Elizabeth was filled with the
Holy Spirit.

Luke 1:41

Hail ✝ Mary

She gave a loud cry and said, 'Of all
women you are the most blessed,/
and blessed is the fruit of your womb.'

Luke 1:42

Hail ✝ Mary

'Yes, blessed is she who believed/
 that the promise made her by the Lord
 would be fulfilled.'

Luke 1:45

Hail 🕊 Mary

And Mary said: 'My soul proclaims the
 greatness of the Lord and my
 spirit exults in God my savior;/
 because he has looked upon his lowly
 handmaid.'

Luke 1:46-48

Hail 🕊 Mary

'Yes, from this day forward all genera-
 tions will call me blessed,/
 for the Almighty has done great
 things for me.'

Luke 1:48, 49

Hail 🕊 Mary

'Holy is his name,/
   and his mercy reaches from age to
    age for those who fear him.'

Luke 1:49, 50

Hail ✠ Mary

'He has shown the power of his arm,/
   he has routed the proud of heart.'

Luke 1:51

Hail ✠ Mary

'He has pulled down princes from their
   thrones/
   and exalted the lowly.'

Luke 1:52

Hail ✠ Mary

'The hungry he has filled with good
   things,/
   the rich sent empty away.'

Luke 1:53

Hail ✠ Mary

Glory be to the Father ∼

Third Joyful Mystery
THE NATIVITY
Our ✳ Father

Now while Mary and Joseph were in
    Bethlehem/
  the time came for her to have her
    child.

Luke 2:6

Hail ✳ Mary

And she gave birth to a son, her first-
    born,/
  and she wrapped him in swaddling
    clothes.

Luke 2:7

Hail ✳ Mary

And she laid him in a manger/
  because there was no room for them
    at the inn.

Luke 2:7

Hail ✳ Mary

In the countryside close by there were
    shepherds/
  and the angel of the Lord appeared
    to them.

Luke 2:8, 9

Hail ✳ Mary

'Do not be afraid. Listen, I bring you
    news of great joy,/
  a joy to be shared by the whole
    people.'

Luke 2:10

Hail ✳ Mary

'Today in the town of David a savior
    has been born to you;/
  he is Christ the Lord.'

Luke 2:11

Hail ✳ Mary

'Glory to God in the highest heaven,/
  and peace to men who enjoy his favor.'

Luke 2:14

Hail ✳ Mary

And some wise men came from the east,/
and going in they saw the child with
his mother Mary.

Matt 2:1, 11

Hail ✳ Mary

And falling to their knees they did him
homage./
Then they offered him gifts of gold
and frankincense and myrrh.

Matt 2:11

Hail ✳ Mary

And Mary kept in mind all these things/
and pondered them in her heart.

Luke 2:19

Hail ✳ Mary

Glory be to the Father, and to the Son,
and to the Holy Spirit./ As it was
in the beginning, is now,
and ever shall be,
world without
end. Amen.

Fourth Joyful Mystery
THE PRESENTATION
Our ✡ Father

Observing the Law of Moses, they took
Jesus up to Jerusalem/
to present him to the Lord.

Luke 2:22

Hail ✡ Mary

Now in Jerusalem there was a man named
Simeon./
He was an upright and devout man.

Luke 2:25

Hail ✡ Mary

It had been revealed to him by the Holy
Spirit that he would not see death/
until he had set eyes on the Christ
of the Lord.

Luke 2:26

Hail ✡ Mary

And when the parents brought in the
      child Jesus, he took him into his
      arms/
  and blessed God.

Luke 2:27, 28

Hail ✡ Mary

'Now, Master, you can let your servant
      go in peace,/
  just as you promised.'

Luke 2:29

Hail ✡ Mary

'Because my eyes have seen the salva-
      tion/
  which you have prepared for all the
      nations to see.'

Luke 2:30, 31

Hail ✡ Mary

'A light to enlighten the pagans/
  and the glory of your people Israel.'

Luke 2:32

Hail ✡ Mary

And he said to Mary his mother, 'You
see this child: he is destined for
the fall and for the rising of many
in Israel,/
destined to be a sign that is rejected.'

Luke 2:34

Hail ✡ Mary

'And a sword will pierce your own soul
too—/
so that the secret thoughts of many
may be laid bare.'

Luke 2:35

Hail ✡ Mary

And they went back to Nazareth, and
the child grew to maturity, and
he was filled with wisdom;/
and God's favor was with him.

Luke 2:39, 40

Hail ✡ Mary

Glory be to the Father ∼

Fifth Joyful Mystery
THE FINDING OF JESUS IN THE TEMPLE

Our 🔲 Father

When Jesus was twelve years old, they
went up to Jerusalem/
for the feast of the Passover.

Luke 2:41, 42

Hail 🔲 Mary

When they were on their way home,
the boy Jesus stayed behind in
Jerusalem/
without his parents knowing it.

Luke 2:43

Hail 🔲 Mary

They went back to Jerusalem looking
for him everywhere./
Three days later, they found him in
the Temple.

Luke 2:45, 46

Hail 🔲 Mary

He was sitting among the doctors,/
    listening to them, and asking them
      questions.

Luke 2:46

Hail 🔲 Mary

And all those who heard him were as-
    tounded/
    at his intelligence and his replies.

Luke 2:47

Hail 🔲 Mary

'My child, why have you done this to
    us?/
    See how worried your father and I
      have been, looking for you.'

Luke 2:48

Hail 🔲 Mary

'Why were you looking for me?/
    Did you not know that I must be busy
      with my Father's affairs?'

Luke 2:49

Hail 🔲 Mary

But they did not understand/
  what he meant.

Luke 2:50

Hail ⛩ Mary

He then went down with them and came
    to Nazareth/
  and lived under their authority.

Luke 2:51

Hail ⛩ Mary

And Jesus increased in wisdom, in stat-
    ure, and in favor/
  with God and men.

Luke 2:52

Hail ⛩ Mary

Glory be to the Father, and to the Son,
  and to the Holy Spirit./ As it was
    in the beginning, is now,
      and ever shall be,
        world without
          end. Amen.

39

First Sorrowful Mystery
THE AGONY IN THE GARDEN
Our 🖉 Father

Jesus came with them to Gethsemane./
And sadness came over him, and great
distress.

Matt 26:36, 37

Hail 🖉 Mary

Then he said, 'My soul is sorrowful to
the point of death./
Wait here and keep awake with me.'

Matt 26:38

Hail 🖉 Mary

Then he withdrew from them,/
and knelt down and prayed.

Luke 22:41

Hail 🖉 Mary

'Father, if you are willing, take this
  cup away from me./
  Nevertheless, let your will be done,
  not mine.'

Luke 22:42

Hail 🖋 Mary

Then an angel appeared to him,/
  coming from heaven to give him
  strength.

Luke 22:43

Hail 🖋 Mary

In his anguish/
  he prayed even more earnestly.

Luke 22:44

Hail 🖋 Mary

And his sweat fell to the ground/
  like great drops of blood.

Luke 22:44

Hail 🖋 Mary

Then he came back to his disciples and
found them sleeping,/
and he said, 'So you had not the
strength to keep awake with me
one hour?'

Matt 26:40

Hail Mary

'You should be awake,/
and praying not to be put to the test.'

Matt 26:41

Hail Mary

'The spirit is willing,/
but the flesh is weak.'

Matt 26:41

Hail Mary

Glory be to the Father, and to the Son,
and to the Holy Spirit./ As it was
in the beginning, is now,
and ever shall be,
world without
end. Amen.

Second Sorrowful Mystery
THE SCOURGING AT THE PILLAR

Our 🕊 Father

They had Jesus bound and handed him
over to Pilate./
Pilate questioned him, 'Are you the
king of the Jews?'

Mark 15:1, 2

Hail 🕊 Mary

Jesus replied, 'Mine is not a kingdom
of this world;/
but yes, I am a king.'

John 18:36, 37

Hail 🕊 Mary

'I came into the world for this: to bear
witness to the truth;/
and all who are on the side of truth
listen to my voice.'

John 18:37

Hail 🕊 Mary

'Truth?' said Pilate, 'What is that?';/
and with that he went out again to
the Jews and said, 'I find no case
against him.'

John 18:38

Hail 🐦 Mary

'So I shall have him flogged and then
let him go.'/
Pilate then had Jesus taken away and
scourged.

Lk 23:16; Jn 19:1

Hail 🐦 Mary

Despised and rejected by men,/
a man of sorrows.

Isaiah 53:3

Hail 🐦 Mary

Harshly dealt with, he bore it humbly,/
like a lamb that is led to the slaughter-
house.

Isaiah 53:7

Hail 🐦 Mary

Yet he was pierced through for our
faults,/
   crushed for our sins.

Isaiah 53:5

Hail ❧ Mary

Ours were the sufferings he bore,/
   ours the sorrows he carried.

Isaiah 53:4

Hail ❧ Mary

On him lies a punishment that brings
us peace,/
   and through his wounds we are healed.

Isaiah 53:5

Hail ❧ Mary

Glory be to the Father, and to the Son,
and to the Holy Spirit./ As it was
in the beginning, is now,
and ever shall be,
world without
end. Amen.

Third Sorrowful Mystery
THE CROWNING WITH THORNS
Our ⁂ Father

The soldiers led him away to the Prae-
torium./
   Then they stripped him and dressed
   him up in purple.
Mk 15:16,17; Mt 27:28
Hail ⁂ Mary

And having twisted some thorns into a
crown they put this on his head/
and placed a reed in his right hand.
Matt 27:29
Hail ⁂ Mary

To make fun of him they knelt to him/
saying, 'Hail, king of the Jews!'
Matt 27:29
Hail ⁂ Mary

And they spat on him/
    and took the reed and struck him on
      the head.

Matt 27:30

Hail ※ Mary

Then Pilate took some water, washed his
    hands in front of the crowd/
    and said, 'I am innocent of this man's
    blood. It is your concern.'

Matt 27:24

Hail ※ Mary

Jesus then came out/
    wearing the crown of thorns and the
      purple robe.

John 19:5

Hail ※ Mary

'Here is your king,' said Pilate./
    'Take him away!' they said. 'Crucify
      him!'

John 19:15

Hail ※ Mary

'Why, what harm has he done?'/
But they shouted all the louder,
'Crucify him!'

Mark 15:14

Hail Mary

'Do you want me to crucify your king?'/
The chief priests answered, 'We have
no king except Caesar.'

John 19:15

Hail Mary

So Pilate, anxious to placate the crowd,/
handed him over to be crucified.

Mark 15:15

Hail Mary

Glory be to the Father, and to the Son,
and to the Holy Spirit./ As it was
in the beginning, is now,
and ever shall be,
world without
end. Amen.

Fourth Sorrowful Mystery
THE CARRYING OF THE CROSS
Our ♦ Father

'If anyone wants to be a follower of
mine,/
let him renounce himself.'

Luke 9:23

Hail ♦ Mary

'And take up his cross every day/
and follow me.'

Luke 9:23

Hail ♦ Mary

And carrying his own cross/
they led him out to crucify him.

Jn 19:17; Mk 15:21

Hail ♦ Mary

And they seized on a man, Simon from
    Cyrene,/
    and made him shoulder the cross and
    carry it behind Jesus.

Luke 23:26

Hail 🐚 Mary

'Shoulder my yoke/
    and learn from me.'

Matt 11:29

Hail 🐚 Mary

'For I am gentle/
    and humble in heart.'

Matt 11:29

Hail 🐚 Mary

'And you will find rest for your souls./
    Yes, my yoke is easy and my burden
    light.'

Matt 11:29, 30

Hail 🐚 Mary

Large numbers of people followed him,/
    and of women too, who mourned and
    lamented for him.

Luke 23:27

Hail 🐚 Mary

But Jesus turned to them and said,
        'Daughters of Jerusalem, do not
        weep for me;/
    weep rather for yourselves and for
        your children.'

Luke 23:28

Hail 🐚 Mary

'For if men use the green wood like
        this,/
    what will happen when it is dry?'

Luke 23:31

Hail 🐚 Mary

Glory be to the Father ∼

Fifth Sorrowful Mystery
THE CRUCIFIXION
Our ✝ Father

When they reached the place called The
  Skull,/
  they crucified him.

Luke 23:33

Hail ✝ Mary

Jesus said, 'Father, forgive them;/
  they do not know what they are doing.'

Luke 23:34

Hail ✝ Mary

One of the criminals crucified with him
  said, 'Jesus, remember me/
  when you come into your kingdom.'

Lk 23:39, 42; Mk 15:32

Hail ✝ Mary

'Indeed, I promise you,' he replied/
  'today you will be with me in para-
    dise.'

Hail ✝ Mary

Near the cross of Jesus stood his
    mother/
  and the disciple he loved.

Hail ✝ Mary

Jesus said to his mother, 'Woman, this
    is your son.'/
  Then to the disciple he said, 'This
    is your mother.'

Hail ✝ Mary

And from that moment/
  the disciple made a place for her in
    his home.

Hail ✝ Mary

And a darkness came over the whole land,
    and the earth quaked;/
   and the veil of the Temple was torn
    in two.

Lk 23:44; Mt 27:51

Hail ✝ Mary

And Jesus cried out in a loud voice,/
   'Father, into your hands I commit my
    spirit.'

Luke 23:46

Hail ✝ Mary

And bowing his head/
   he breathed his last.

Jn 19:30; Lk 23:46

Hail ✝ Mary

Glory be to the Father, and to the Son,
   and to the Holy Spirit./ As it was
    in the beginning, is now,
     and ever shall be,
      world without
       end. Amen.

First Glorious Mystery

THE RESURRECTION

Our ✿ Father

'I tell you most solemnly, you will be
    sorrowful,/
  but your sorrow will turn to joy.'

John 16:20

Hail ✿ Mary

'For I shall see you again, and your
    hearts will be full of joy,/
  and that joy no one shall take from
    you.'

John 16:22

Hail ✿ Mary

At the first sign of dawn, they went
    to the tomb/
  with the spices they had prepared.

Luke 24:1

Hail ✿ Mary

And all at once the angel of the Lord,
descending from heaven,/
came and rolled away the stone and
sat on it.

Matt 28:2

Hail 🕊 Mary

'I know you are looking for Jesus, who
was crucified./
He is not here.'

Matt 28:5, 6

Hail 🕊 Mary

'He has risen from the dead./
Come and see the place where he lay.'
Lk 24:6; Mt 28:6, 7

Hail 🕊 Mary

'And now he is going before you to
Galilee;/
it is there you will see him.'

Matt 28:7

Hail 🕊 Mary

And the women came out from the tomb/
filled with awe and great joy.

Mk 16:8; Mt 28:8

Hail 🔖 Mary

'I am the resurrection and the life./
If anyone believes in me, even though
he dies he will live.'

John 11:25

Hail 🔖 Mary

'And whoever lives and believes in me/
will never die.'

John 11:26

Hail 🔖 Mary

Glory be to the Father, and to the Son,
and to the Holy Spirit./ As it was
in the beginning, is now,
and ever shall be,
world without
end. Amen.

Second Glorious Mystery
THE ASCENSION
Our 🙟 Father

Jesus took them out as far as the out-
    skirts of Bethany,/
  and lifting up his hands he blessed
    them.

Luke 24:50

Hail 🙟 Mary

He said, 'All authority in heaven and
    on earth/
  has been given to me.'

Matt 28:18

Hail 🙟 Mary

'Go, therefore,/
  make disciples of all the nations.'

Matt 28:19

Hail 🙟 Mary

'Baptize them/
    in the name of the Father and of the
    Son and of the Holy Spirit.'

Matt 28:19

Hail ✿ Mary

'And teach them to observe/
    all the commands I gave you.'

Matt 28:20

Hail ✿ Mary

'He who believes and is baptized/
    will be saved.'

Mark 16:16

Hail ✿ Mary

'He who does not believe/
    will be condemned.'

Mark 16:16

Hail ✿ Mary

'And know that I am with you always;/
   yes, to the end of time.'

Matt 28:20

Hail ⚜ Mary

As he said this he was lifted up,/
   and a cloud took him from their sight.

Acts 1:9

Hail ⚜ Mary

And so the Lord Jesus was taken up into
   heaven:/
   there at the right hand of God he
   took his place.

Mark 16:19

Hail ⚜ Mary

Glory be to the Father, and to the Son,
   and to the Holy Spirit./ As it was
   in the beginning, is now,
   and ever shall be,
   world without
   end. Amen.

Third Glorious Mystery

THE DESCENT OF
THE HOLY SPIRIT

Our 🟦 Father

When Pentecost day came around,/
they had all met in one room.

Acts 2:1

Hail 🟦 Mary

Suddenly they heard what sounded like
a powerful wind from heaven,/
the noise of which filled the entire
house.

Acts 2:2

Hail 🟦 Mary

And something appeared to them that
seemed like tongues of fire;/
these separated and came to rest on
the head of each of them.

Acts 2:3

Hail 🟦 Mary

They were all filled with the Holy
    Spirit,/
  and began to speak about the marvels
    of God.

Acts 2:4, 11

Hail 🕊 Mary

Now there were devout men living in
    Jerusalem/
  from every nation under heaven.

Acts 2:5

Hail 🕊 Mary

And Peter stood up with the Eleven/
  and addressed them in a loud voice.

Acts 2:14

Hail 🕊 Mary

'Repent and be baptized,/
  and you will receive the gift of the
    Holy Spirit.'

Acts 2:38

Hail 🕊 Mary

And they accepted what he said and
were baptized./
That very day about three thousand
were added to their number.

Acts 2:41

Hail Mary

Send forth your Spirit, and they shall
be created;/
and you shall renew the face of the
earth.

Pentecost Alleluia

Hail Mary

Come, Holy Spirit, fill the hearts of
your faithful:/
and kindle in them the fire of your
love.

Pentecost Alleluia

Hail Mary

Glory be to the Father ∼

Fourth Glorious Mystery
THE ASSUMPTION
Our ❀ Father

'Come then, my love,/
   my lovely one, come.'

Song 2:10

Hail ❀ Mary

'For see, winter is past,/
   the rains are over and gone.'

Song 2:11

Hail ❀ Mary

'Show me your face, let me hear your
      voice;/
   for your voice is sweet and your face
   is beautiful.'

Song 2:14

Hail ❀ Mary

And the sanctuary of God in heaven
opened./
  Then came flashes of lightning and
  peals of thunder.

Rev 11:19

Hail ❀ Mary

Now a great sign appeared in heaven:/
a woman, adorned with the sun.

Rev 12:1

Hail ❀ Mary

She was standing on the moon,/
  with the twelve stars on her head for
  a crown.

Rev 12:1

Hail ❀ Mary

With jewels set in gold, and dressed in
  brocades,/
  the king's daughter is led in to the
  king.

Psalm 45:13, 14

Hail ❀ Mary

May you be blessed, my daughter, by
    God Most High,/
  beyond all women on earth.

Judith 13:23

Hail ❀ Mary

The trust you have shown shall not pass
    from the memories of men,/
  but shall ever remind them of the
    power of God.

Judith 13:25

Hail ❀ Mary

You are the glory of Jerusalem! You
    are the great pride of Israel!/
  You are the highest honor of our
    people!

Judith 15:10

Hail ❀ Mary

Glory be to the Father, and to the Son,
and to the Holy Spirit./ As it was in the
beginning, is now, and ever shall be,
world without end. Amen.

Fifth Glorious Mystery
THE CORONATION
Our ✳ Father

Who is this arising like the dawn,/
   fair as the moon, resplendent as the
      sun?

Song 6:10

Hail ✳ Mary

Like the rainbow gleaming against bril-
   liant clouds,/
   like blossoms in the days of spring.
Ecclus 50:7, 8

Hail ✳ Mary

'I am the rose of Sharon,/
   I am the lily of the valleys.'

Song 2:1

Hail ✳ Mary

'My throne is in a pillar of cloud,/
  and for eternity I shall remain.'

Ecclus 24:4, 9

Hail ☀ Mary

'Approach me, you who desire me,/
  and take your fill of my fruits.'

Ecclus 24:19

Hail ☀ Mary

'I am like a vine putting out graceful
  shoots,/
  my blossoms are sweeter than honey.'

Ecclus 24:17, 20

Hail ☀ Mary

'And now, my children, listen to me;/
  listen to instruction and learn to be
  wise.'

Prov 8:32, 33

Hail ☀ Mary

'Happy are those who keep my ways,/
who day after day watch at my gates.'
Prov 8:32, 34

Hail ✳ Mary

'For those who find me find life,/
and win favor from the Lord.'
Prov 8:35

Hail ✳ Mary

Hail, Queen of mercy, protect us from
the enemy,/
and receive us at the hour of death.
Queenship of the B.V.M., Gradual

Hail ✳ Mary

Glory be to the Father, and to the Son,
and to the Holy Spirit./ As it was
in the beginning, is now,
and ever shall be,
world without
end. Amen.

79

Hail, Holy Queen, Mother of Mercy, our life, our sweetness, and our hope! To you we cry, poor banished children of Eve; to you we send up our sighs, mourning and weeping in this valley of tears. Turn then, most gracious advocate, your eyes of mercy toward us; and after this our exile, show to us the blessed fruit of your womb, Jesus. O clement, O loving, O sweet Virgin Mary:

℣. Pray for us, O holy Mother of God.

℟. That we may be made worthy of the promises of Christ.

In the name of the Father, and of the Son, and of the Holy Spirit./ Amen.

The *Scriptural Rosary* book is also available in Spanish, German, French and Italian. In English there is a dramatized cassette set.